FOR TEENAGERS ONLY

FOR TEENAGERS ONLY

BY

BRYAN H. REED

METHODIST YOUTH DEPARTMENT
PAGES LANE,   LONDON, N.10

FIRST PUBLISHED IN 1958
Reprinted 1959, 1960

© THE EPWORTH PRESS 1958

Book Steward
FRANK H. CUMBERS
FOUNDRY PRESS, LTD., BEDFORD

PRINTED IN GREAT BRITAIN BY
FOUNDRY PRESS LTD. BEDFORD

CONTENTS

CONTENTS

1. GROWING UP

Have you ever played at 'Baby-Spotting'?—everybody produces a photograph of himself in infancy, the pictures are then arranged round the room and the prize goes to the person who makes the largest number of correct identifications.

It may not be quite as hilarious, but it is certainly very amusing to compare the photograph of a boy or girl at thirteen or fourteen with a photograph of the same individual at nineteen or twenty. It is difficult to believe that one is looking at likenesses of the same person.

So many things are crowded into these few short years of the teens. At thirteen Johnnie is a schoolboy, always untidy, usually dirty (often in trouble for not washing behind his ears), interested in comics this week, engine-spotting the next, and in collecting badges the week after that. Eight or nine years later he is just completing his National Service, he may have been half round the world, he knows exactly what the Prime Minister ought to do about Egypt or Cyprus (or whatever is in the headlines at the moment). He has become a *man*.

At thirteen his twin sister is a schoolgirl with pig-tails and ankle-socks, given to fits of the giggles, and, maybe, making her first experiments with lipstick with rather alarming results. And eight or nine years later? She is perhaps going steady with a boy-friend, perhaps engaged to be married, maybe even married, but certainly interested in furniture shops, colour schemes, household budgeting and bathing the baby. She has become a *woman*.

It has been said that the chief business of the adol-

7

escent is to stop being one, and certainly most of you are in a tremendous hurry about it.

Not that this business of growing up is very easy. It is a bit embarrassing when one's familiar body takes on unfamiliar shapes and one is always dropping things or tripping over things because one's feet or hands somehow suddenly get out of control; it is still more upsetting when one is disturbed by all sorts of new, exciting, but rather frightening feelings and emotions.

One difficulty is that you are never quite sure whether you are supposed to be grown-up or not. If you had been born into a primitive aboriginal tribe you would have been required, at a certain age in your early teens, to go through an initiation ceremony when you would pass in one step from childhood to adulthood. One day you would be a child, subject to parental control and discipline, and the next day you would be a recognized adult, free to set up a home, to start a family, to fight or hunt or dig, and to take your place in the councils of the tribe.

In our country today there is no such clear transition from one stage of development to the next. You may, if you so wish, leave school at fifteen; you can't drive a motor-bike till you are sixteen or a motor-car till you are seventeen. Until you are seventeen, too, the police regard you as a juvenile; if you are a boy you are called up for National Service at eighteen (or, you were, before conscription was abolished), but you can't vote until you are twenty-one. Just exactly when do you become grown-up?

Mums and Dads don't always help. In one breath they refuse to allow you adult privileges and in the next complain that it is high time you accepted a bit more responsibility. They seem to want it both ways.

And yet how exciting these teen-years are. The great choices are still open, the pattern of your life is still to be decided. You can still choose what you are going to be, what you are going to do with your life, whom you will marry, what causes you will serve, what gods you will worship.

But you haven't much time. If you become a grocer you can't be an engineer, and if you marry Jane you can't marry Elizabeth; the choices you make in the next year or two will shape the rest of your life, as long as you live.

It would seem, therefore, to be mere common sense to make the right decisions now. The chapters that follow are intended to help you to do so.

2. BRINGING UP MUM AND DAD

Not so very long ago, in the sands of Egypt, there was discovered a letter written, it is supposed, about three thousand years ago, in which the writer grumbled that 'young people aren't what they were; they no longer obey their parents'.

It is obviously a very old complaint. Even in the best regulated families there are occasional arguments between one generation and the next—arguments about latch-keys or lipstick, about boy-friends or pocket-money, or about the use of Sunday or holidays-without-the-family.

Or perhaps Mum comes home one day to discover that her daughter Mary has been moving the furniture around or taking the pictures down ('Nobody has pictures nowadays, Mum!'), and realizes with something of a shock that there is another woman in the home. And when there are two women in the same house . . .

If I were writing here, not to you, but to your parents, I would at this point want to say that we parents must learn to let go. You youngsters grow up so quickly, you know, that it really is hard for us to keep up to date with you. We nearly always think of you, not as you are now, but as you were six months ago. And so much has happened to you in the last six months. It is always later than we think.

We don't find this 'letting-go' very easy, of course. It is more difficult for Mum than for Dad. After all, he still has his job to worry about. But for the last fifteen or sixteen years you have been Mother's 'job'. Her whole life, pretty well, has been looking after you. (You might remember that, you know.) And now she feels that her whole life's work is slipping away from her.

Most youngsters pass through a phase, in their middle teens, when they don't tell their parents everything. I imagine, for instance, that most girls don't tell their mothers about their first love-affair, though they may tell the Sunday-school teacher or the club leader or the minister's wife. And Mum, of course, is terribly upset. 'Why should Mary tell Mrs Jones and not me'. But of course, Mum is the one person in the world Mary can't tell, not because she doesn't love her any more, but because Mum is the person who has controlled her life for so long that it is just at that point that Mary feels in her bones that she has to assert her growing independence. And if Mum is wise she will understand, and won't ask a whole lot of questions, but will be content to wait. If she is unwise she will try to hold on to Mary too tightly too long, and run the risk, maybe, of an estrangement that may be hard to heal.

But I am not writing for your parents, but for you (though, if you like, you can let them read the last three paragraphs). And there are two things I want to say, to you.

First, you might remember sometimes that we were here first. We may not be any more intelligent than you are. (Psychologists tell us that we never become more intelligent than we are at sixteen and a half, so that at that age you may well be quite as intelligent as your parents. What comes after that is an increase of knowledge and experience, but no increase of native ability.) But, as I say, we were here first—not quite as long ago as the days of Queen Victoria or the period of antimacassars and aspidistras, but still, quite a while ago. It does mean, don't you think, that because we have lived a bit longer we have more experience of life; we do know where some of the dangerous corners are, we remember some of the mistakes we made. And if it doesn't sound too sentimental to say so, we do love you, you know (more perhaps, than you guess), and the advice we give you, which may sometimes seem to you so antique, and even the prohibitions upon which we insist just occasionally (to your very great indignation), may have their origin in our care for you. Please believe that what we say may be worth listening to and thinking about.

Second, you might remember, too, that you won't have us always. You had better make the most of us while you've got us. It is a pity to be out every night. How many evenings did you spend at home last week ? Have some of your fun at home. Go places with the family. And instead of taking the girl-friend to the pictures next Friday, give her a miss for once and take Mum instead—and your girl-friend, if she is the right sort, will respect you all the more for it.

And if, in your home, there is occasional friction or even quarrelling, you might ask yourself how much of it is your fault, and whether there is anything you could do about it. A happy home is so priceless a blessing, that it is worth making every possible adventure in reconciliation to achieve it.

Postscript. Oh, there is one other thing. You've probably had a better education than your parents ever had. They're proud of you, of course, but just a bit sensitive, sometimes, about their ignorance of things which you know all about (or do you?). The most

11

unpleasant people on earth are the snobs, and the worst snob of all is the fellow who is ashamed of his own parents—parents who, for all their lack of book-know-ledge, may have more wisdom in their little fingers than he has under his hat — to say nothing of a hundred times more grace. Don't forget.

3. THE FIRST PAY PACKET

A red-letter day, never-to-be-forgotten, is the day when we come back with our first pay-packet. This is how one writer describes the feeling one has on such a day:

'The work is likely to be much harder than at school, but is worth paying any price for what seems to be freedom. To be able to buy cigarettes and to spit; to cheek the foreman (at least once), to dream of the backchat you'll give the boss, to go to the pictures with your own money, to swagger on the monkey-parade with your own girl. You have watched it enviously through the school bars and now you are free to expand in it like a butterfly in the sunshine.'

For many of you, no doubt, it was not like that at all, but it is a tremendous event in a fellow's life when he leaves school behind him and joins the ranks of the world's workers. Judging by appearances, too, it is even more important in the life of a girl. One week she is a (more or less) demure schoolgirl in gym tunic and pigtails, and the next time you meet her she's 'something in the city' in stiletto heels, nylons, ear-rings, a new hair-do and lipstick of vivid hue. In both cases, a very long step forward in the growing-up process has been taken.

It would be interesting to know how you choose your first job.

Not many years ago there was a good deal of juvenile unemployment, and in some of the depressed areas it happened that men grew to adult-hood without ever having been offered the chance of any job at all. You may have seen the problems of such people portrayed in the film or stage version of 'Love on the Dole'. During the same period there were a good many blind-alley jobs—jobs where one was automatically sacked at eighteen, having acquired no skills or qualifications since leaving school at fourteen.

Those days, happily, are past. Everybody seems to want you—there is a scarcity of juvenile labour—and a wide range of possibilities is open to you. The ideal job, of course, is the one in which you get paid for doing what you would want to do anyway, and, to help you to come to a decision, you have the expert and disinterested advice of the Youth Employment Service, which is quite prepared to tell you how to become an air hostess or a fashion buyer, a deep-sea fisherman or a mining engineer.

If you are a young Christian the decisive consideration will be, not the size of the pay packet, the prospects of promotion, the cushyness of the job or the amount of the pension, but the will of God.

Yes, the will of God. If God is as interested in us as the Bible and the Christian religion says He is, there can be few questions with which He is more concerned than our choice of a life's job, and He calls some people to be bank clerks or bus drivers just as certainly as He calls others to be preachers or doctors. If we sincerely seek His will and are ready to be guided by Him, His will becomes clear to us. I don't mean, of course, that we shall hear voices in the night, or that messages will appear on the bedroom ceiling, but if we are genuinely prepared to be guided by Him, then when decisions have to be made, it will be clear to us what we should do. And, as a wise man said long ago, in His will is our peace. Nowhere else, indeed, is there satisfaction or peace of mind.

It is, perhaps, worth adding a word about full-time Christian service. Such a call does not come to us all, but we do need more Ministers, Deaconesses, workers on the Mission Field (especially doctors, nurses and teachers), and people to staff our Children's Homes. Have you thought about this? Have you prayed about it, too?

Most of you, however, will find yourselves in offices, shops or factories. Some such places will offer very happy and helpful surroundings in which to work, but there is no getting away from the fact that often the general standards of personal relationships are pretty poor, conversation rather smutty, and it is considered clever to diddle the firm or the boss. If your religion means anything at all, it is up to you to uphold those standards you know to be right. What our country needs as much as anything is more men and women of transparent integrity—people whose lives are as pure as a thread of wool, as clean as a grain of salt, and as white as a flake of snow.

But you mustn't become a prig, and there's no need to walk about labelled 'holy' all over. We have to maintain our standards without compromise, but to do so in charity and tolerance and with great good humour. The only people we shall ever influence are people we truly love.

We can't achieve all this off our own bat, of course, but the whole point of the Gospel is that God Himself can do in us what we could never do for ourselves. He comes to the immediate help of one who prays. Try Him and see.

4. SPARE TIME

'Oh, but I've got no time!' How often we use those words. But they are not always true, are they? Just think how much time there is. There are 168 hours in every week. Of these we probably spend fifty-six in bed, forty at work and twenty-one at our meals, which still leaves us with fifty hours or so, most of which we can probably use pretty much as we wish.

Some of you, of course, are spending long hours at your homework or at evening classes of one sort or another, while others have taken on jobs in connexion with Church activities. All honour to you—your free time may be quite a bit less than fifty hours a week.

One recent writer, by no means unsympathetic to youth, remarks that young people never had more money or more leisure than they have today, and that on the whole they don't know what to do with either. And there are lots of fellows and girls, you know, of whom that is true. Young people come in for a lot of criticism, and most of it is undeserved (just because a small handful of Teddy Boys make a general nuisance of themselves, there is no need to make foolish generalizations about the 'increase of juvenile delinquency'), but what is true is that there are far too many young people today whose lives are pretty empty and dull and purposeless—who have hardly read a book since they left school, who have no skills, hobbies or enthusiasms, who hold no great beliefs and serve no great causes. Their lives are marked by boredom rather than by any positive wrongdoing. They don't know how to use their leisure time.

There are two main ways of using spare time—we can sit back and be entertained by other people, going to the pictures, watching our favourite team, sitting in

15

front of the TV; or we can do something ourselves, playing games, pursuing hobbies or settling down with a book.

There's nothing wrong, of course, about 'canned' entertainment, so long as we don't allow it to steal too much of our leisure. But there is something unbalanced about things when a fellow goes to the pictures two or three evenings a week or sits glued to the TV night after night. Of course, the way you spend your leisure is bound to be affected by the nature of your everyday work. If you are sitting at a desk all day you will need some sort of exercise in your free time, but if you are a bus conductress you will be like one eighteen-year-old girl I knew who wrote that when she had a free evening she wanted to 'stope in'.

Do find some time for some sort of active and creative use of at least some part of your leisure. Here we are, living in this beautiful world, heirs of all the ages, with the best literature in the world in the public library not far away, and unless you live in the very remote country, opportunities for following almost any kind of conceivable skill or hobby, whether it is bee-keeping, orchestral music or car maintenance, kindly laid on for you by a generous Local Education Authority or University Extra-Mural Department. There is no excuse for boredom; there need never be a dull moment. Boys need not be cabbages and girls need not be shop-window dummies. Go places; study the history of your own town; take an interest in politics, science, art, literature, music, religion. Don't become one of those poor dim-wits whose interests hardly stagger above comic strips and football pools. There is no need, in this twentieth century, to live as though printing had never been invented or a musical notation not yet devised. Forget about seaside land-ladies, save the money you spend on smoking in twelve months, and spend your next holidays cycling in Brittany or walking in the Pyrénées.

Two things in particular. First, get out of doors. You might start with an ordnance survey map of your own area, and then, with the map, explore the footpaths, woods and hills. Know the wild flowers, trees, birds and fish of your own district. Learn to find your way by the stars; know how to swim. If you've got a bike, use it to appreciate the countryside.

Second, do something for other people. There is so much you could do — baby-sitting for young married couples, shopping or gardening for old-age pensioners, putting on a show in the local hospital, entertaining children whose names will gladly be given you by the local Children's Officer, reading to blind people, offering hospitality to coloured folk in your neighbourhood—not to mention the job that's waiting for you in your own church or Sunday-school. Write down on a piece of paper just how you spent your fifty free hours last week, and show it to God when you say your prayers.

5. YOUTH ORGANIZATIONS

Unless you live in a very remote hamlet, there are probably a good many youth organizations within reasonable reach of your home, most of which would be ready to welcome you as a new member.

It is surprising, really, to discover how many different types of youth group exist. I made a list, once, of all the teen-age societies to be found within the Birmingham City boundaries; I got up to 1,384, and even then I dare say there were a good many others I never heard about.

They are of all sorts, too: uniformed and non-uniformed, mixed and single-sex, political, industrial, sporting, religious and pre-Service—everything from prayer meetings to rock n' roll. They meet in all sorts of places, too — schoolrooms, church halls, barns, garages, lofts, and, very occasionally, specially built and equipped club premises.

But in spite of all these opportunities lots of you never join any of them. In England and Wales rather less than half the teen-age boys and not more than a third of the girls belong to any kind of group or society at all. Many join a club but soon drift away—perhaps this was the fault of the club, perhaps it was the fault of the new member, who perhaps hardly gave the club a fair trial.

Why do people join a club, anyway? If someone asked you why you go to your club I dare say you would reply: 'I go because my friend goes' or 'I go to meet my pals.' And a very good reason, too. After all, when you come to think about it, a club is a sort of half-way house between the home where you were brought up as children and the wider world where you are pretty much under the authority of the boss. In the club you are part of a society of people of your own age. There you have a place of your own, you can run your own show, plan your own activities, organize your own committees and raise and spend your own funds. Like the fellow who didn't know that he had been speaking prose all his life, you, without perhaps ever giving it a thought, have been trained for democracy.

When you argue things out in committee, and accept and act on a majority decision which went against you, you are preparing yourself for service, later on, in the local Town Council or even at Westminster. That's why the most useful youth organizations (in my opinion, anyway) are the mixed ones, where fellows and girls meet together in committee to plan the activities of their own society, and where the members really do run their own show and are not merely 'organized' by some adult 'leader'. You will need a grown-up leader, of course, but if he is wise he will give you lots of rope and be content to lead from behind.

Once you see that the main purpose of a club is just to be a society of young people of similar age (if I wanted to be really highbrow, I would say 'to help its members to achieve social maturity', which merely means to learn how to live and work with other people in a civilized way) you will be on the look-out to help new, awkward or shy members to feel at home. They are probably the very people who most need what the club can give them.

Then, of course, the club will need a programme. If it is an 'Independent' club its main activities may be games or sports; if it is run by the Local Authority there will probably be a number of formal classes (Drama, Crafts, P.T., and so on); if it is one of the uniformed organizations there will be a very rigid scheme of training to follow; and if it is associated with a church there may well be all these things plus—and it is a very big plus—opportunities for religious education, for worship, and for service to the community around.

I visited a club once where one of the rules was 'Politics and Religion barred' but there is hardly any question you can discuss which does not, in the end, go back to a political or religious issue. What on earth is the use of the club where you are not allowed to talk about the most important questions of all? The King George's Jubilee Trust, in an immensely important Report published not long ago, said: 'We believe that work with young people must be founded on the Christian ethic and the recognition of Christian standards of thought and behaviour.'

Remember that a club must have a programme. No club will last long on table-tennis, darts, and billiards. Members of such a club will soon get bored and drift away. The clubs which hold their members are those which insist on certain standards, and which really do offer a balanced programme—something to do, something to enjoy, something to make, and something to think about; activities for the summer, for the winter, for indoors and outdoors; for boys, for girls and for mixed groups; not forgetting the occasional high-light or red-letter day (the Annual Dinner, the Summer Camp, the Christmas Pantomime), and not forgetting, either, that some form of specific service to the local community ought to be a high priority in the work of any self-respecting youth group.

And one last word. Remember that a youth organization is a youth organization. It is something, not only to join, but also to leave. Unless you remain as a leader you have no business at all in a youth organization when you have passed your teens. You ought by then to have moved on to some more purposeful adult society. The aim of a youth organization is to help you to grow up, not to keep you young too long.

6. BOY MEETS GIRL

It happens to most people as they reach the teens that they awake to a new and exciting interest in members of the opposite sex. This is natural and right and proper—it is how God made us. It is a sign that the people concerned are growing up.

It cannot be said too strongly that sex in itself is beautiful and clean and holy. It is not something about which to snigger or whisper in dark corners or about which to tell suggestive stories or smutty jokes. It is God-given and, rightly used, can bring some of the greatest joys which life can offer. Unfortunately some of our parents were themselves so inhibited about this subject that they left us in ignorance about what are sometimes called the facts of life, and left us to pick

20

up the information we wanted from other, and sometimes unhealthy, sources.

Remember, though, that while sex is important, it is not the only thing in the world. You are living in a time when sex is being flung at you—often in suggestive ways—in films, newspapers, magazines, advertisements, hoardings. It would almost seem that it is impossible to advertise anything—from holidays to tooth-paste—without putting a half-undressed girl in the picture. The fault with so many films is not that they are immoral or indecent—in spite of the 'daring' posters outside—but that often their whole attitude to life is so false and untrue. It is taken for granted in many films that the only possible relationship between a man and a woman is a sentimental, romantic one. And that, of course, is just not true. The man and woman joint leaders of your Youth Club probably work together in close and intimate partnership, but without the slightest suggestion of romance in their relationship. On your Club Committee, too, you think, argue and plan together in complete disregard of sex differences. One of the main purposes of a mixed club, indeed, is to help its members to attain mature, adult and sensible relationships with members of the opposite sex.

The films are liable to lead you astray, too, because so often they assume that the only basis of marriage is that of physical attraction. And again they are wrong. Of course, good looks do enter into it, but the real foundation of a happy marriage is not to be found in a neat ankle or a Roman nose (if it were, the marriages of film-stars would be the most lasting of all), but in the virtues of consideration, understanding, patience, humour, forgivingness, fidelity and mutual respect.

Sex is holy and clean. Keep it that way. It can go bad on you. It is a tremendously powerful instinct, and once it gets out of control it can very easily carry you away to disaster. Some people have their biggest

21

battles with themselves just at this point, and here, too, many a good man has gone wrong.

Your interest in sex is perfectly natural, but there are too many people in Britain and America who make money by trying to exploit your natural interest in sex by its titillation in all sorts of unhealthy and suggestive ways—music hall nudity and near-pornographic publications. It is both sensible and Christian not to expose oneself to this sort of contamination. There are certain Sunday newspapers and illustrated weeklies with which we would be wise never to soil our minds.

Sometimes it happens that boys and girls—because of ignorance—don't play fair with each other. A girl doesn't always know that a boy's passions are more quickly aroused than her own, and that, once aroused, they are more difficult to control. Boys don't always know that intimacies which to them mean little or nothing can stir a girl to her depths and leave her profoundly distressed.

Yes, sex is holy and beautiful. Keep it that way. It is natural and indeed desirable that fellows and girls in their teens should mix, that they should get to know one another, do things together, and form friendships with each other. But don't let it go farther than that until you are quite sure of each other. The rule is that one should never use a person of the opposite sex as a mere means of physical stimulation or excitement. Such a relationship is bound to be destructive of mutual respect and to lead to remorse, disgust, and self-contempt.

In spite of what so many modern play-wrights say, the standards of Christian sexual morality — chastity outside marriage and fidelity within marriage — were not invented by a lot of narrow-minded old fogies who were shocked at the suggestion of anything else; they are principles which generations of men and women have found to point the only way either to personal

22

happiness or to social health. They are rooted, of course, in the will and purpose of God.

Infidelity in marriage may sound very funny in a cheap music hall joke; it is not at all funny if one of the people involved is your sister or your mother.

7. MARRIAGE OR CAREER?

This, of course, is a chapter for girls, but there is no reason why boys should not read it—to do so indeed may perhaps help them to understand their girl-friends better.

There are a good many injustices in life, and there's no doubt about it that girls have to face one enormous problem from which boys are spared. Boys can look ahead, plan their careers and pursue their ambitions, but for girls there is always uncertainty—a future on the one hand as wife and mother, or on the other as independent wage-earner or professional woman.

It can be a very real problem, even for girls in the middle teens. 'Am I to stay at home four or five evenings a week, studying for professional examinations, or shall I go to the training-class or tennis club or Mrs Smith's party, where men are to be met?'

Except in that minority of families where there is a tradition that children continue their education up to university level, it is often almost assumed that a girl will have had two or three boy-friends by the time she is seventeen, will be 'going steady' at eighteen or nineteen, and is considered a social success if she is married in her early twenties. How then can she promise to be at the club drama group every Wednesday or the church choir every Friday, when, to quote Miss Pearl Jephcott: 'If a boy should whistle she must be free to go to him.'

All this, of course, may be very flattering to any boys who read this chapter—it is very flattering to think that one's company is so much desired—and equally annoying to girls, who naturally like to think of themselves as the pursued rather than as the pursuers.

Well, of course, boys are quite capable of doing their own share of pursuing, but there is something very 'off-putting' both about boys who can think of nothing but girls, and about girls who can think of nothing but boys. As this is a chapter for girls, however, I should like, even though I am a mere man, to tell them that while their interest in boys is perfectly healthy and right and proper, no girls are more despised than those who throw themselves at boys. I remember a friend once saying to me: 'Helen came to the club to find a boy-friend—an excellent place to find one, too—but she made it so obvious, and wondered why teen-age boys avoided her as much as juniors avoid soap and water.' Never let yourself become 'cheap'.

Marriage or a career? But, many of you will want to ask, why not both? Can I not combine marriage and a job? Of course you can. Many married couples nowadays find it necessary for the first few years of married life that the wife should continue to earn. How else, indeed, can you save up enough to pay for the home and furniture.

I can't help feeling, however, that this arrangement should not be allowed to continue too long. No home is complete without a family; a baby car is a poor substitute for a baby in the pram, and a couple are wise if they start a family while they themselves are as young as possible. Then—whatever may be right for childless wives—a mother's place is surely in the home. To bring up children is not only a full-time job; there is no more important or worthwhile work in the world.

I said in the last chapter that sex is important, but that it isn't the only thing in the world. The same

24

kind of comment may be made about getting married. To marry happily, to bring children into the world, and to build a truly Christian home is one of the very greatest blessings that life can give. But should it be that marriage does not come to you, you must not feel that you are a failure or allow yourself to become rebellious or embittered; it is still possible to live a full, rich, useful and victorious life. Far, far better, indeed, never to marry, than to marry the wrong person.

One thing we might all do is to avoid cheap, unkind and cruel jokes about 'old maids'. Many of the finest women I know are unmarried. Denied the love of husband and children, they nevertheless face life with gallantry and courage, and spend themselves in the service of other folk. How much we owe them, and how poor we should be without them!

8. MONEY

In some parts of the country it is customary for a young wage-earner to bring home his wage-packet and to hand it to his mother unopened. She buys his clothes and is responsible for all important expenditure, but hands him back a certain amount of pocket-money for himself.

It is good, of course, that youngsters should realize their debt to the family and their responsibility toward younger children, but I can't think that this custom is good. It would be better training for the fellows or girls concerned to pay mother as generously as possible for board and lodging but to take responsibility for buying their own clothes and meeting their own bills.

Some older people complain that you youngsters have far more money than is good for you and that you don't know how to use it wisely. Such feelings, after all, are very natural. It is not many years since a good many men had to keep a whole family on no more than some of you are spending on tobacco or gramophone records, and though nobody loves a miser, some of you might be wise to throw your money about a little less freely than you do. Lots of marriages have run into early difficulties when both partners have found that they could no longer afford the expensive habits of bachelor days. Smoking, for instance, can be a shocking waste of money. The cost of thirty cigarettes a day, if saved and invested, would produce a thousand pounds in ten years' time.

It is wise, too, to be wary of those people who want to sell bicycles, TV sets and radio-grams on the Never-Never. Sometimes, of course, hire-purchase can be a very great help, and when you want to buy a house of your own you will no doubt enlist the help of a Building Society, but don't get involved in weekly payments beyond your ability to pay. Better, and cheaper, to save first and pay cash.

Thrift is not a popular virtue and lots of people try to live beyond their income in a frantic effort to keep up with the Joneses. But it is both patriotic and sensible to put something by regularly, and it is his plain duty, when a fellow marries, to take out an insurance policy on his own life, so that, in the event of his own early death, his widow and children will not be entirely penniless.

It is only sensible, too, to have nothing to do with gambling in any form. It is a mug's game, anyway; why should we enrich bookmakers and football pool promoters? Gambling, too, is a complete reversal of the movement toward the abolition of extremes of wealth and poverty which is one of the glories of the Welfare State. (How any Socialist can indulge in gambling beats me!) It is a complete denial, too, of any conception of Christian stewardship.

Yes, Christian stewardship. A Christian believes

that all he has—including his time and his money—is lent to him by the Lord. Our time and our money belong to God. That doesn't mean, of course, that we can never spend an hour in sheer frivolity or money in occasional personal extravagance. It does mean, however that at the end of the week we ought to be able to present both the week's diary and the week's cash accounts to the Lord without any sense of shame. An increasing number of Christian people are tithing their income (i.e. giving a tenth of it to God), but whether we do that or not we certainly ought not to spend more in any one week in amusements and tobacco and cosmetics and sweets than we offer to the Lord for His work. Just how much are we offering Him?

I said, a couple of chapters back, that sex was important, but that it wasn't the only thing in the world. The same can be said about money. There's a dreadful Yorkshire saying: 'Ees nubbody, 'ee 'as nowt'—dreadful, because it is sheer snobbery to judge people, not by what they are, but by what they chance to possess. It was said of St Francis, when a lad in his father's shop, that one day a rich merchant and a beggar entered the shop simultaneously, and that Francis was most embarrassed because he didn't know which to attend to first. He was blind to the fact that one was rich and the other poor—to him they were just two men, both claiming his attention. We may not easily attain to such Christian perfection, but in this St Francis was one with our Lord.

It is worth remarking, too, that all the best things in life cannot be bought, and that all God's greatest gifts are without money and without price.

9. NO MORE CALL-UP

We are all glad to know that at long last compulsory National Service is being brought to an end in Britain. For most fellows it has been something they would rather have been without, while for those who have had to follow long professional studies it has sometimes meant that they have been half-way through their twenties before they have been able to take their final exams.

It is a pity that National Service has had a military character and purpose. If only the world could be delivered from the fear of war there might be something to be said for a period of universal National Service in which fellows and girls of all social levels could work together in peaceful enterprises. One thinks of slum clearance, road construction, afforestation and coastal defence as possible projects in which young fellows could add to our national heritage by the labour of their hands. Here is a topic for your next Club discussion or debate: Would you be in favour of some such compulsory National Service for all, and what forms of service would you suggest for girls?

The ending of conscription means that young fellows are no longer compelled, at eighteen or thereabouts, to make the hard choice between joining one of the Services or registering as conscientious objectors. At the same time there are still very good reasons why each of us should make up his mind just where he stands on this issue.

Some Christians will feel that the nature of modern war is such that they cannot possibly have any active participation in it and must therefore register as conscientious objectors. The sheer horror of the hydrogen bomb makes such a point of view very understandable. If war comes to mean the annihilation of

28

whole populations (the appalling slaughter and suffering of Hiroshima and Nagasaki on a continental scale) it is difficult to see how those who acknowledge divine authority for the New Testament could ever sanction the use of such weapons.

On the other hand there will be those who feel with equal sincerity that there is nothing in the Christian religion which forbids us to kill wicked men when they are bent on evil, even if it means destroying multitudes of innocent people at the same time, that love itself is neither weak nor sentimental but may be firm and strong, and that in a sinful world the possession of force is necessary to preserve that law and order without which civilization itself would be destroyed and all progress made impossible.

It is an awful dilemma, and whichever opinion we hold we ought to be sufficiently aware of the strength of the other point of view to make us humble and tolerant in our attitude toward those from whom we differ.

Whatever our personal views, however, we are living in a world of heavily armed nations where for some time to come we are likely to retain an Army, a Navy and an Air Force, and a certain proportion of young Christians will find themselves serving in one or the other.

There is no doubt about it that if you do enlist in one of the Armed Services, your character will be subjected to a pretty searching test. If you are sharing a barrack-room with thirty other fellows they will soon discover what sort of chap you are, and it will quickly be apparent how firmly based your standards are.

It is important to nail one's colours to the mast straight away—to say one's prayers, to read the Bible, to go to Church. You'll be ridiculed a bit, of course, at first, but in their hearts fellows will respect you and before long some of them will be asking you questions about your religion and, maybe, taking their stand with you. There are ministers of religion today whose interest in Christ began when they met Christians in the Forces. And if you are a Christian it is a good thing to seek out the Padre straight away—he is there to help you and he will welcome your help. It is important, too, to link up with a local Church wherever you are—you are almost sure to get the warmest of welcomes and to make new friends of the right sort.

It is a queer thing that when people get together in a crowd there is often a general lowering of standards all round. A crowd can be far more cruel than any of its individual members, a group of quite decent men can start telling smutty stories, half a dozen perfectly nice women can exchange the most malicious gossip. So sometimes in the Forces. But there is no need to join in the sexy stories (you won't believe half of them, anyway), and if you are sensible enough to be a tee-totaller there is no need to start drinking beer just because some others do so; there are lots of perfectly reasonable and sensible arguments for total abstinence.

10. 1066 AND ALL THAT

Some time before *Picture Post* ceased publication a fifteen-year-old girl wrote to the Editor complaining that he was devoting too much of its space to politics and speeches 'and such dull-like things' and not enough to films and variety. It occurred to me, when I read that letter, that had it not been for the 'dull speeches' of people like Lord Shaftesbury and others years ago, that girl would have had neither leisure nor ability to write letters to the Press; she might have been working as much as sixteen hours a day six days a week in factory or even in mine for three or four shillings a week.

Whatever may be the correct answer to the stock debating question: 'Is the world getting better or worse?' Britain today is a much better place in which to grow up than it was a quarter of a century ago or more. Never was more done for young people (or for older people, too, for that matter). The State, through its Ante-Natal clinics, is interested in you before you arrive among us; while you are children the State again is concerned about your health, your home-life, your education; and as you pass into the teens the State steps in again with its interest in your employment and in your leisure. Even in your short lifetime English Social History has been made in important legislation dealing with Child Care, Education, Youth Service, National Health, Social Security, and Youth Employment.

As a matter of fact we in this country are in the middle of an enormously important social experiment. We are accomplishing a silent revolution — without bloodshed and without violence. We are seeking to abolish extremes of wealth and poverty, to give every child equal educational opportunities, to make medical treatment promptly available to every man, woman and child, and above all to remove from every home the haunting fear of poverty, unemployment and want. We are building the Welfare State. And lest any of you should think that here I am introducing party politics, it can be said that all three main political parties in this country have contributed to what we have done, and none of them would ever dare to put the clock back.

If we succeed in what we are attempting we shall have accomplished something unique in the history of the human race on this planet—to have built, without violence, a social order based on principles of brother-hood, freedom, tolerance and respect for the rights of

31

minorities. You can call it, if you like, Social Democracy, or the Welfare State, or the Western Way of Life. If we succeed, we shall be envied by all other peoples and we shall earn the praise of historians of the future. 'If we succeed.' Because, quite frankly, we may quite possibly fail. I am thinking here, not of the danger of external attack or of possible involvement in an American-Russian war, but rather of internal collapse. Many a civilization in the past has fallen, not because of the attacks of its enemies, but through internal decay.

The fact is that there are far too many of us who want all the benefits of the Welfare State without its responsibilities. There are far too many sectional interests scrapping with each other for the biggest possible share of the national cake, too many of us are lazy and work-shy and generally irresponsible. We forget that every penny given back to us in education or health service, sick benefit or family allowance, has first to be earned by somebody—and earned, too, in a highly competitive world in whose markets we are increasingly undercut by other nations where people work longer hours and are content with a lower standard of life than is to be found among us.

The simple fact is that we shall only save the Welfare State if we are prepared to do an honest day's work for a day's pay. We ought to look on all our work in the world—whatever it is—not only as a way of earning money, but as our service to the community, our contribution to the creation of a Democratic Society.

Democracy is not just one among many possible methods of Government, nor is it something which we can take for granted; it is something in which to believe, of which to be mighty proud, something that deserves our loyalty and our service.

Do you remember the words which Her Majesty the Queen broadcast on the evening of her Coronation?

This is what she said: 'There has sprung from our island home a theme of social and political thought which constitutes our message to the world . . . Parliamentary institutions, with their free speech and respect for the rights of minorities, and the inspiration of a broad tolerance—all this we conceive to be a precious part of our way of life and outlook. I ask you now to cherish them, and to practise them too; then we can go forward in peace, seeking justice and freedom for all men.'

Perhaps those words do not sound very exciting or urgent. Perhaps the phrase 'Parliamentary institutions' conjures up a picture of a lot of old men half asleep—something less vivid, anyway, than the coloured shirts and military bands with which dictator countries have appealed to their youth—but what we are trying to do here is something far more wonderful even though it may be less spectacular.

Democracy is much more than a system of government; it is a way of life. We practise it whenever we rise above prejudices of class or colour, when we allow other people the right to their opinions. The Trade Unions in this country have an honourable history and have been powerful instruments of social reform, but it is enough to make one weep when, insisting on the right to strike, they deny their members the right not to strike, and victimize men who, for religious or other reasons, refuse to toe the line. It is equally deplorable when Trade Unions call their members out on strike because of rivalries between themselves, or when workers refuse to work alongside coloured people. We need not only to give lip service to Democracy but to practise it in our relations with our fellows.

This chapter is already far too long, but there is one more thing to be said. It is a simple historical fact that this democratic way of life derives from New Testament teaching about the Fatherhood of God and the brotherhood of man, and will only be secure as it continues to derive its inspiration from the same source. We do not preach Christianity because it contributes to peace and prosperity, but because it is true. Nevertheless if the teaching of Christ were to cease among us, it would not be long before civilization reverted to the jungle. In your short lifetime we have seen what terrible things men will do to one another in gas chambers and concentration camps when they abandon belief in the God and Father of our Lord Jesus Christ.

11. LIVING ON A LARGE MAP

How much interest do you take, I wonder, in what is told us in BBC News Bulletins or in the newspapers about what is being said and done by people in New York or Moscow, Geneva or Tokyo? What do you know about political tensions between Greeks and Turks in Cyprus, or about French troubles in Algeria?

The difficulty, I know, is that some of these places seem so far off and that so often we seem unable to do much about things anyway. We seem at times the helpless victims of vast forces which toss us about like corks on a stormy sea. Nobody wants another war, but we are all piling up new and dreadful weapons. We are just in the position of St Paul when he said that the good that he would he did not, and the evil that he would not, that he did.

In the meantime there are lots of other things to think about—there is a smashing film on at the local cinema this week, and a new variety show on TV tomorrow. What responsibility is it of ours if children in Central Africa or somewhere are dying of hunger, and what could we do about it, anyway?

Whether we like it or not we are involved in what

happens to other people all over the planet. We live in One World. Political unrest in India or Japan could at once produce unemployment in Lancashire, while if war breaks out anywhere in the world we are at once affected.

And if there is any meaning at all in the brotherhood of man, ought it not to concern us that there are still millions of refugees and displaced people in the world, that in South Africa and elsewhere coloured people suffer exploitation and injustice solely on account of race, that in the United States of America the average annual income of every man, woman and child is 1,500 dollars, but in India it is only twenty-five dollars, and that half the human race is both illiterate and hungry and is indeed born to lifelong poverty and want?

But what can we do about it? Here are four suggestions.

First, we can take an interest in world affairs. There are broadcast talks and newspaper articles which can keep us in touch with what is happening in the world. In some Youth Clubs the leader gives a regular quarter-of-an-hour summary of the events of the week; and lest this sounds deadly dull—it need not be—mention can be made of sporting events and scientific discoveries as well as of speeches and conferences. There is everything to be said, too, for inviting political speakers to your club, provided that equal opportunity is given to each party. It is also worth remembering that public opinion is public opinion — made up of the views and ideas of millions of ordinary people. When, in November 1956, the British and French Governments invaded Egypt, it was the immediate upsurge of public opinion in our own country and throughout the world that compelled an almost immediate reversal of policy. If the ideals of the United Nations are to be achieved, it will only be as millions of us believe in the United Nations, talk it up, and support its actions, even if at times they appear to run counter to our own national pride.

Secondly, we can do all we can to promote goodwill in our own contacts with people from overseas. We can avoid every form of colour prejudice; we can go out of our way to offer friendship to students and workers from overseas. What about a 'Guest Night' at your Youth Club, with invitations to overseas people in the locality?

Thirdly, it is worth remembering that there is no more valuable contribution to the peace of the world than that which is being made by the Missionary Societies of the Churches. Doctors, nurses, teachers, preachers and social workers go out from our own land to work side by side with Christian leaders of the countries to which they go. Long ago it was said of a missionary doctor on the north-west frontier of India that he was worth a couple of regiments. Of course he was; it is far better to win the friendship of your enemy than to try to hold him down by force. You may not be called to become a missionary yourself (though are you quite sure about that?), but there are many ways in which your own Missionary Society needs your help, and its work is surely the most important in the world.

Lastly, if you are a Christian, try to bring a Christian judgement to every political, industrial, and international question. Being a Christian doesn't just mean feeling all 'gooey' on Sunday nights, or singing a lot of sentimental religious choruses round a piano; it also means finding out what is involved in following Christ in this world here and now. It means relating the teaching of the New Testament to questions like the closed shop, secret commissions, restrictive practices in industry, unofficial strikes, marriage and divorce, work and leisure.

36

12. WHAT ABOUT COMMUNISM?

It is quite absurd, of course, to try to say anything about so vast a subject as Communism (which can mean so many different things) in a mere page or two. At the same time Communism cannot possibly be ignored, if only because it is the most serious rival Christianity has ever had to face, and because our very lives may depend upon our relationships with Communist countries over the next few years.

The extraordinary spread of Communist influence in this country has been amazing. When Karl Marx was buried in Highgate cemetery in 1884 a dozen mourners attended his funeral; today his teachings are regarded as Gospel by hundreds of millions of people. There is hardly a country anywhere in Europe or the Far East which hasn't got its active Communist Party. We ought to avoid hysterical and emotional wholesale condemnation of Communism as though all Communists were nasty bogey-men or fifth-columnists from Hell. It is only fair to remember that while there is much in Communism that is evil, Capitalism, too, has very often deserved the judgements of God. We should remember too, that in Russia, China, Poland and elsewhere there are Churchmen who find it perfectly possible to be both Christians and Communists. Christianity is by no means to be equated with the American way of life.

The whole attraction of Communism is that it does appeal to what is visionary and idealistic within us. Communism looks at the world and sees all its poverty, its hunger, its illiteracy, and says: 'It's our job to change all that: nothing is impossible; there are only degrees of difficulty.'

It is not surprising therefore, that its doctrine of

37

racial equality should appeal to coloured people the world over, and that its demand for social justice should attract deprived and dispossessed people everywhere. It would be hard not to be a Communist, perhaps, if one lived in one of the Near Eastern Arab States where there are a handful of people who are fabulously and disgustingly wealthy, while the great mass of the population lives in hunger, want and wretchedness.

If any of you, however, are tempted to become Communists, you are doomed to a terrible disillusionment. If Communists accept the teaching of Marx they cannot believe in God; nor do they believe that there is any ultimate standard of Truth or Right to which we must all give allegiance. It follows that lies, torture and murder become virtues if they serve the interests of the Party. Communism therefore maintains itself in power by the most appalling cruelties, by secret police, brain-washing, and concentration camps. The individual counts for nothing; political rivals are arrested, tortured, made to 'confess' and finally are 'liquidated'. Families are broken up, any criticism of the régime is visited by the most appalling punishment, there are Party spies everywhere, scholars and writers are not allowed freedom of thought, and whole populations are kept in ignorance of what is happening in the outside world. The fact is that the splendid idealism of many people all over the world is being exploited in the interests of tyrannical imperialist dictatorship.

It is the fundamental error of Communism that it believes that there is an economic remedy for all our troubles. If only we could abolish poverty, it says, we should have a Paradise on earth. We must do all we can, of course, to abolish poverty (and in this country at least we are rapidly doing that), but when we have achieved this desirable aim, other and greater problems will still remain. Our troubles stem, not only from 'the system', but from within ourselves — from pride, fear, envy, in fact from all seven deadly sins — and I guess they are just as evident in Moscow as they are in London or New York. Communism complains that religion offers pie in the sky when you die; but what Communism offers is pie in the year 3000 or so for the lucky people alive then, but nothing for people living now. Christianity says that the Kingdom of God is already here, and that all who wish to do so can enter in right now. When Karl Marx lived in London his little boy died of hunger and privation. For weeks Karl Marx was prostrate with grief; there is nothing in Communism to heal a father's broken heart.

What we must never forget, however, is that Communism might never have arisen if Christians had been more concerned about social justice. Communism thrives on hunger, unemployment, and racial prejudice. The rest of us have far too long tolerated inequalities which cannot be reconciled with a belief in the Father-hood of God and the brotherhood of man. Too many of us, in spite of our Christianity, still cling to privilege, are still class-conscious, or will not accept coloured people as social equals.

A century or so ago Christians roused the conscience of the country about the injustices suffered by over-worked children and exploited factory workers in our own midst; it is our task, in this new age, to keep before our minds that half the human race on this planet is born to lifelong poverty and want, and that there can be no enduring peace in the world while such con-ditions persist.

It is not enough to condemn Communism; we must out-think it and out-live it. We must minister to our needy brethren—on the material level, yes; but also on those deeper levels where Communism has nothing at all to give.

13. DOES RELIGION MATTER?

Several times, in these pages, there have been references to religion, but we have not yet squarely faced the challenge of the all-important question: 'Is religion going to have any place in my life, and if so, what sort of place?'

I know there are people today who take the view that religion is an optional extra, a rather high-brow hobby perhaps, like ballet or opera—interesting, no doubt, to people who like it, but of no importance to those who don't. Or they think of it, perhaps, as something that happened to people who wore queer clothes in Palestine a long time ago, and it never remotely occurs to them that religion belongs also to this world of films and football, rock and rockets, skiffle and sputniks. Still less do they realize that religion may have something to say about the things in which they really are interested, jobs and pay-packets, sport and leisure, home and friends.

But the very first assertion which religion makes is that God is a Living God, active and speaking, at work here and now; still more, that He is our Father, who knows us all and loves us, and is more eager to help than ever we could be to seek His help.

If this is true—and the only way, finally, to prove its truth is to put it to the test—it is surely foolish, to say the least, to go through life without the guidance and inspiration, the strength and comfort which religious faith could give.

It is perfectly true, of course, that some people seem to manage very well without religion; we all of us know some perfectly delightful people who don't appear to have the slightest interest in religion but who live satisfactory lives nevertheless. The fact is that while we can manage for a certain length of time—and sometimes for quite a long time — without the help of religion, sooner or later we find ourselves in a situation where only religion can help us, and where, without it, we shall be bankrupt and helpless indeed. This moment may come to us in an experience of utter loneliness when all our friends have failed us, in a time of bereavement, of failure, of hopelessness, or, it may be, in a day when we see as in a blinding flash what rotters we are and how desperately we need cleansing and empowerment. 'Oh wretched man that I am,' exclaimed St Paul, 'who shall deliver me?'

The fact is that all the deepest needs of our nature are religious needs, and can only be satisfied by religion. We want to feel that we matter, and the only real assurance comes from the knowledge that we are the children of God; in this very dangerous world we need security, and the only possible guarantee of that is in the faith that this is God's world; we want to know what is right and what is wrong, and again the answer is in the will of God; we want power, not merely to recognize what is right, but to do it, and this empowerment is one of religion's greatest gifts. (A bit stiff—this last paragraph. It's a very important one—read it again.)

Religion is not only a list of great beliefs, nor is it a way of life only. It *is* these things, but above all it is a transforming experience. The real difference between the religious man and the other fellow is that the religious man, if he has got the real thing, has found resources of power and courage which the other fellow, thoroughly good chap though he may be, just knows nothing about. The religious man is in touch with God, and all the powers of God flood into his life; he has found the secret of victorious living.

I put it to you that the most important questions you will ever have to face are questions like these: Am I

41

going to seek and to do the will of God? Am I going to live as a child of God?

Don't evade these questions. Don't postpone an answer to them. Don't sit on the fence. Come clean. Make your decision about them, once and for all. Now.

14. JESUS CHRIST

In the last chapter we were thinking about religion, but religious people do not normally talk about 'religion' any more than a lover talks about 'girlhood'. He talks about Mary or Joan or whatever her name is. In the same way religious people talk, not about religion, or even about Christianity, but about Jesus Christ.

To all Christians religion means the experience of fellowship with Jesus Christ. Before trying to explain what this means, however, it is worth pointing out that I am not implying that other religions are full of nothing but evil or error. There is no doubt some measure of truth and virtue in them all. In the Christian religion, however, we find the goodness and truth and beauty of which all other religions are limited and partial expressions.

Don't be put off by the fact that Christianity is presented to us in many different dresses, and that there are even in your town or village many different denominations. His Holiness the Pope, Dr Billy Graham and Dr Donald Soper would differ on many questions, but they agree far more than they differ; they read the same Bible, sing the same hymns and serve the same Lord. As for the different denominations, there is far more unity among them than many people believe: they are like different regiments in one army.

Don't be disturbed, either, because you once heard

of a parson who ran off with the choirmaster's wife. There are, after all, millions of Christians in the world, and no doubt some of us are poor advertisements of our religion. The best of them, however—and you can be quite certain of this—are the finest people in the world. If you want to know what Christianity really is, you must look, not at the poorest specimens you have known, but at the best—and above all, you must look at Jesus Christ.

And the very least that can be said about Him is that His was the noblest life ever seen on this earth; He was the greatest Man who ever lived, there never was a life in which courage and purity and love were so perfectly united. He has influenced the course of human history more than all the kings and parliaments and armies of the world all put together.

Religion, I said just now, is the experience of fellowship with Jesus Christ. That, after all, is how it began— a group of a dozen young fellows — very ordinary chaps too, most of them, who gathered round their Leader, a Leader who so won their love and loyalty that most of them, in the end, willingly laid down their lives for Him. And so, for most of us, the Christian life usually begins as a personal loyalty to Jesus Christ.

But it does not stop with that; it goes on to become a growing experience of what Christ can do for us. Let me just mention three things.

First, He answers our questions. All of us, sooner or later, want to know what God is like, why He created us, what life is for, why evils like suffering should exist, and whether we may look forward to a life after death. To all these questions Jesus has an answer. The Christian religion is not just a sentimental 'Let's kiss and be friends'; it sets forth a number of great convictions, articles of faith, which are embodied in the historic creeds of the Church. Christ Himself said: 'I am the Truth.'

Secondly, He shows us the way. What sort of people should we be? What kind of character should we desire? By what rules should we govern our relationships with one another? How do we know, a girl once asked, that what we call right is right, and what we call wrong is wrong? Where, in other words, do we find our standards of conduct and behaviour? To all these questions the answer is to be found in the life and example and teaching of Jesus Christ. He said of Himself: 'I am the Way.'

Lastly, He empowers us. Not only does He point us the Way; He carries us along it. What Christians have found all down the centuries is that through commitment to Jesus Christ they are able to accomplish what otherwise would be quite beyond them. The most characteristic thing about a Christian is not what he believes or how he behaves, but what has happened to him—he has found a new power, a new peace, a new purpose. The New Testament sometimes calls this experience 'salvation', and elsewhere it speaks of it as 'eternal life', or as 'finding the kingdom of God'. These phrases all refer to the same thing—the experience of victorious living which is the hallmark of the Christian in every age and place. To be saved is just to be fully and completely alive. Jesus Himself said: 'I am the Life.'

15. H BOMB OR KINGDOM COME

It is no more than simple fact to say that the human race has reached a turning-point in its history. We have come to the place where we have to make the ultimate choice. We now hold in our hands atomic powers of quite unimaginable magnitude. Used for peaceful and constructive purposes these powers could make possible progress, advance and achievement that would transform the conditions of human life on this planet. If, on the other hand, thermo-nuclear weapons were used in a third World War, our towns and cities would be wiped out and millions of people would perish in fearful suffering. The horrors of such a disaster do not bear thinking about. Some scientists believe that the mere testing of nuclear weapons, if continued, will produce changes in the atmosphere which will do untold harm to generations of children as yet unborn.

Is there any hope for us? Can we look into the future with any confidence at all? To what may we look forward—to what one bishop has described as the 'plague' of the H Bomb, or to an answer to our daily prayer that God's will shall be done, and His Kingdom come, as in Heaven, so on earth?

Some people pin their hopes to education, some to the United Nations and international agreements, others to military pacts and alliances, while others again suggest that if only we could get rid of the present Government and put in a new one, then Utopia would soon be here.

All these suggestions, no doubt, are of value, but it is only too obvious that none of them can save us. Education may increase our skills; it cannot guarantee that we shall use our knowledge wisely. History is littered with solemn international treaties which have often proved worth less than the paper they were written on. Those who pin their faith in military alliances should be warned that the greatest dangers at the moment arise from the fact that so many nations are lined up in opposite armed camps. As for a change of Government, we should surely have learned by this time that all the laws in the world, however excellent, cannot by themselves create the Kingdom of God. In the year 1789 in France 632 Deputies were instructed to draw up a constitution which would guarantee to all men liberty, equality, fraternity. They were given a fortnight in which to complete their task; but France has her troubles still.

The real truth is that we need more Christians in the world. It is as simple as that. And by Christians I mean not just nominal adherents, but people whose private lives and personal relationships are altogther ruled by the mind and spirit of Jesus Christ.

During the second World War, Haile Selassie, Emperor of Abyssinia, was driven from his country by Mussolini, the Italians invading his land with bayonets and poison gas in one of the most unjustified and unprovoked aggressions of modern times. When the war was over and the Italians were defeated, Haile Selassie was able to return to his own country, and his first act was to arrange a solemn Thanksgiving Service in his Cathedral. He himself preached the sermon, in the course of which he said: 'There must be no revenge upon the Italians who remain in our midst; we must show them how Christians forgive.' Can anyone doubt for a moment that if men of that spirit and temper were in authority in all the nations, there are no problems which trouble us today which could not rapidly be solved.

Those of you who live in the Midlands may be familiar with the Selly Oak Colleges — a group of a dozen different institutions, of different denominations, but all engaged in training young men and women for various forms of Christian service at home or overseas. Among the three hundred students living there at any one time will almost certainly be found Americans and Chinese, Germans and Scandinavians, men and women from behind the Iron Curtain, men and women from all the five continents, and of every shade of colour. Different in nationality, in background and outlook, different in denomination and in theology, they enjoy a rich fellowship together; they are one in Christ. Their life together is practical evidence of the

46

truth of words spoken by William Temple: 'As though in preparation for such a time as this, God has raised up a fellowship which now extends into almost every nation in the world and binds citizens of them all together in unity and mutual love. It is the great new fact of our time. It is the one ground of hope for the future.'

Three things are blazingly clear.

First, in our personal relationships with one another we must be ruled by the spirit and temper of Christ. We cannot pretend to tell other people how they should conduct their relationships if we ourselves are bullying, intolerant, selfish, or if we habitually 'look down' on people of different colour, race, occupation or education. Christian relationships begin in the home, in the office, in the shop . . .

Secondly, we need rapidly to increase the number of Christians in the world. There may not be much time left. Evangelism was never more urgent or important. And if the idea of yourself as an evangelist is rather startling, you can begin quite simply by telling your mate at work that you have become a follower of Christ, and why.

Lastly, we must join the Church and do all we can to deepen the fellowship its members have with one another. The Church is not a continuation committee brought into being to propagate the teaching of Christ; it is itself part of the Gospel—the living demonstration in a world torn by fear and suspicion of the fellowship which all men can and do find in their common loyalty to Jesus Christ.

16. MAKE UP YOUR MIND

In the last three chapters we have tried to see why people can't do without religion, we have thought about the offers and claims of Jesus Christ, and we have seen how literally and urgently true it is that Christ is the Hope of the world.

If you agree with what has been said in these three chapters (and, quite honestly, I can't see how anyone could disagree), the next step is in your own hands and not in mine. What are you going to do about it? It is quite useless to agree theoretically and vaguely that Christ is the Hope of the world; it is quite another thing to enlist unreservedly in His service. We are each of us confronted with a personal challenge to which no one but ourselves can respond. Does what has been written lead you to the point where you are prepared to make an absolute Christian decision?

I know, of course, that very few people become Christians because they have become intellectually convinced of its truth. It is much more like falling in love. A fellow doesn't draw up a schedule of what he is looking for in his future wife—ten marks for cooking, ten for neatness, ten for cheerfulness, and so on—and then make a list of all the girls he knows to see who gets the highest marks. No, he probably falls in love with a girl who might get quite poor marks, but he is quite sure, nevertheless, that she is the finest girl in the world.

In much the same way most people become Christians. Perhaps they were brought up in a Christian home, or they came under the influence of a Christian man or woman, or they joined a Youth Club and got caught up in its Christian fellowship, or perhaps they caught a glimpse of Jesus Christ, and that was quite enough to bind them to Him for life. And so, in a hundred different ways, people have begun the Christian life, and they have found the 'reasons' afterwards.

Not that 'reasons' are unimportant. God wants us to love Him not only with our feelings, but with all our minds. We need never fear the truth. For two thousand years Christianity has withstood the most critical and searching inquiry, and will no doubt continue to do so.

The experience of becoming a Christian is what is known as 'conversion'. This involves much more than a personal decision on our part—though that, of course, is quite essential—it implies also the total transformation of life which takes place when Christ is really put at the centre of things. It includes not only what we do in making a decision, but what God does in us when the decision has been made.

For some people conversion is a very sudden dramatic experience, accompanied perhaps by intense emotional excitement and disturbance. But with most people it isn't like that at all. They perhaps could not even say just when they were converted; they could not mention any particular time or place—their whole life has been marked by an increasing dedication to the service of Christ and by a deepening awareness of His presence and power. One sort of conversion, of course, may be just as real and genuine as the other.

Always, however, even in the most 'gradual' of conversions, there must surely come a time when one affirms the decision one has made. One can hardly drift unawares into the Kingdom of Heaven. Sooner or later one must say something like this: 'I don't know exactly just when I began to be a Christian, but I know I am one. I don't know when I first began to follow Christ, but I am committed to Him, once and for all, without compromise or reserve, for time and for eternity. So help me God.'

This decision, once made, must be continually renewed. We need again and again to reaffirm our vows of allegiance. Many Christians find regular attendance at the service of Holy Communion a great help in this way.

It is perhaps worth adding that it could be said of most Christians that they are converted, but not converted enough. In other words, conversion is a progressive experience. Every department of our lives—our home-life, our leisure, our business, our politics, our relationships with the people next door, with the opposite sex, our use of money, and everything else—must all be made subject to Christ. There are many perfectly sincere and genuine Christians who have got 'blind spots' — areas of their lives which, all unconsciously, they have not yet surrendered to Jesus Christ. It is easy and tempting to apply this to people we know; our business is to apply it to ourselves.

Further, whether conversion is sudden or gradual, its results are always the same — not merely a passing emotion or temporary excitement, but an abiding transformation of life and character. The man who is most fully and completely converted is the man who is most Christlike—the man in whom are to be seen the graces and virtues of Christ, and the peace, power, love and joy which are always His gifts to those who commit themselves to Him.

So the next move is yours. If you are one of those people who are attracted to Christ but as yet uncommitted, if your mind agrees that what has been said in these pages is true but as yet you have done nothing about it, may I challenge you to come off the fence? The times are so urgent that there is little use for spectators. If you have not yet made the final commitment of your life to Christ, do it now. Make up your mind. Today is the day. This is it.

To offer one's life to Christ is, of course, the most important step toward living a Christian life, but it is only a step; there is a long journey ahead—a journey full of adventure, achievement and discovery.

We do not make the journey alone, of course, and millions of people have travelled before us. We follow a road trodden hard by the feet of many saints—a road, too, well sign-posted with warnings and directions.

In this and the next chapter or two we think about some of the things which, through the years, people have found quite essential in living the Christian life.

WORSHIP

Worship is to a Christian what petrol is to a car; without it his life is powerless and meaningless.

Most people, I suppose, can remember moments when they experienced a sense of the presence of God. This awareness may have come to them through the beauty of the world around them, through some call to duty or challenge to service, through contact with some noble man or woman, through some more personal experience of great joy or sorrow, or through any one of a thousand other things—but it was a moment when God seemed very near and very real.

What a Christian has to do is to cultivate these moments—to train himself to recognize the many ways of God's coming and speaking to us all, until, in the end, he lives always as in the presence of God.

God is alive, active, and at work. He is far more ready to speak to us than we are to listen, far more eager to help us than we are to accept His aid. There is no situation, either in the world at large or in our own personal lives, beyond His desire and power to remedy. This strong conviction must be at the basis of all effective Christian living. To hear some people talk, one would almost imagine that God was dead. We need first to believe in God, and then continually to realize His presence. In other words, we need a revival of worship.

This is not an appeal for an orgy of emotionalism. Our feelings are in fact one of the least reliable guides to the state of our spiritual health; our loyalty to Christ is to be judged, not so much by our excitement as by our obedience. Very often when we worship our feelings may be quite unmoved. That does not mean that our worship has been ineffective—in fact we never need to worship more than at those times when we least feel like doing so.

Nor is this a plea for uniformity of experience. Some people are helped most by the colour and symbolisms of elaborate ritual, others by the simplicity and silence of a Quaker Meeting, and others again by the warm-hearted singing of the great hymns of the Church. No one approach is better or worse than any others; they are just different, that's all.

What does matter is that we should each find a method of prayer which helps us and meets our needs. Some people find books on prayer quite useful, and one which is helping many teen-agers is *A Prayer Diary for Youth* by L. P. Barnett [1], others again find it a good thing to use their hymn-books for private devotional purpose. But you must make a rule for yourself, setting aside some time every day when, without fail, you recollect the presence of God and seek His will for the day. And, remember, never give up because sometimes it all seems very unreal and difficult.

[1] Published by the Methodist Youth Department, 3s. 6d.

To be an intelligent or effective Christian there are certain facts you must know. The Christian religion sets forth a few quite precise declarations about God, about Jesus Christ, and about ourselves. These declarations are summed up in the Apostles' Creed. You must, therefore, know what this Creed says, and be able to talk about it with a certain amount of understanding.

I know, of course, that no one has to pass an examination before becoming a Christian, and there are lots of perfectly good Christians who are very simple souls and who hold some quite extraordinary beliefs. But we shall all of us be a lot more use to Christ if we use our minds as well as our hands in His service. There are in fact far too many young Christians today who seem to offer Christ everything except their minds—they will spend hours singing rather silly choruses round a piano or travel by the coach-load to emotional religious 'rallies' but will not attend a regular Bible-class or study-group.

What this all means is that we ought to do a certain amount of religious reading, and that we should begin with the Bible itself. The best method is to get a group of half a dozen other people and then ask your minister or someone to lead you—and he will be only too grateful for the chance of doing so. Do see to it that in the programme of your Youth organization there is opportunity for some quite regular study of the Bible for those members who want it.

You'll want to do your own private reading as well, but here too you will need help. The Bible is by no means an easy book to read, and without guidance one can soon become discouraged. The kind of help you want is to be found in daily readings published both by the International Bible Reading Association and by the Bible Reading Fellowship.

It is implied in what is said above that if you are going to continue in the Christian life and to grow in it, you will need the help of other people. But this is so important that it deserves a chapter to itself.

18. THE CHURCH

I wonder if you have heard the story of the man who gave five reasons for never going to the cinema:

1. No one at the cinema ever spoke to him.

2. Every time he went someone asked him for money.

3. The man in charge never visited him.

4. The people who went didn't live up to what the films taught them.

5. His parents took him too often when he was a child.

It is very easy, of course, to find lots of reasons for not going to Church — the imperfections of Church members, the divisions of the Church, the dullness of Church services, and so on. I want to give four reasons why we should join the Church.

First, the Christian religion has been kept alive in the world through the worship and witness of the Church, and would certainly not survive very long if all the churches were turned into cinemas, dance-halls or factories. There are of course some very good people quite outside the Church, but it can usually be said of them that they are as good as they are because of the influence of the Church which they now ignore. Björnson, the Norwegian poet, was also a member of the Norwegian Parliament. One day some of his political opponents threw some stones through the windows of his house, but, before they dispersed, they sang the Norwegian National Anthem, which he had himself composed. His comment was: 'They may smash my windows, but they can't help singing my song.' Many people who try to pull the Church to pieces still sing her song, because the teaching of the Church has become so much a part of themselves.

In one busy London street a building that was once obviously a church is now the head office of a brewery and heavily placarded with liquor advertisements. Does it matter very much? Most people would admit that the world needs more Christianity and not less, and the Church, after all, is the only organization in the world the sole object of which is to promote the Christian religion. The Church may not always be very lively, but it is in fact the Army of God, committed to active campaigning.

Secondly, if we are at all serious in our intention to lead a Christian life, we shall need the help and encouragement of other Christians. In all ages Christians have come together in worship because in worship they have found inspiration and strength.

It is worth remembering that if ever there was One who could have lived without the help of public worship, it was surely our Lord, and yet we read that the sabbath found Him in His place in the village synagogue 'as His custom was'. There were no great thinkers among the preachers at Nazareth, among the worshippers there were some whose hypocrisy was obvious, and the congregation was so snobbish that when Jesus preached His first sermon they could only complain that His father was a carpenter; but Jesus continued to attend week by week. A habit that He found so essential is not likely to be one which we can afford to neglect.

Thirdly, the Church exists, not merely that the Gospel may be preached, individuals converted, children taught, and the sick and the dying comforted, important as all these functions are, but also to give the world an illustration of a new kind of community life— the life of the Kingdom of God. What impressed men about the very first Christian Church was not only the quality of character of its members, but the love they had for one another. The most important sermon any Church has to preach can never be preached by the minister alone; it is the sermon preached by the whole congregation as people are compelled to say about them: 'See how these Christians love one another; here are people who have discovered the secret of fellowship, the secret for lack of which the world is rushing head-long to disaster.' That is what is meant when it is said that the Church itself is part of the Gospel. To be a Christian, therefore, means more than to be a Christlike individual — it means belonging to a Christian community, the Church.

We go to Church to worship God. The old Scottish catechism says that 'the chief end of man is to glorify God and to enjoy Him for ever' and St Augustine said that 'God has made us for Himself and our hearts are restless until they find their rest in Him'. In worship we meet with God and so reach the loftiest heights of which we are capable. It is, perhaps, a crude illustration, but just as a dog in his master's company, will exhibit qualities and virtues which do not appear when he is in the company of other dogs, so we too are at our best when in the conscious presence of God. 'To worship', said William Temple, 'is to quicken the conscience by the holiness of God, to feed the mind with the truth of God, to purge the imagination by the beauty of God, to open the heart to the love of God, to devote the will to the purposes of God.'

It is worth remembering, too, that most members of the Church are in Heaven, and that when we worship in Church we take our place among the gallant company of saints, apostles, prophets and martyrs who through twenty centuries have served their Lord and ours.

'Therefore with Angels and Archangels, and with all the company of heaven, we laud and magnify Thy glorious Name: evermore praising Thee, and saying, Holy, holy, holy, Lord God of hosts, heaven and earth are full of Thy glory: Glory be to Thee, O Lord most High.'

19. ACTIVE SERVICE

You have probably heard the story of the oldest inhabitant who, asked what he did all day long, replied: 'Sometimes I sits and thinks, and sometimes I sits.' Psychologists used to tell us that we each of us live, as it were, on three levels: we think, we feel, and we act. Any worthy religion must embrace all three sides of life—it will involve something to believe, something to feel, and something to do.

'Something to do.' Whole volumes could be written, and have in fact been written about Christian living; but far and away the most important active service to which we are called is the work of evangelism. Every Christian should be an evangelist.

Does that surprise you? Does it perhaps embarrass you? If it does, it may be because you are thinking of evangelism in too narrow terms. Evangelism has not necessarily anything to do with oratory or with mass meetings. An evangelist—to use the word in its strict meaning—is someone who is on to a good thing and finds it so good that he just has to share it with other people.

If it is true that a Christian possesses the secret of a peace, a power, a joy and a love which other people, excellent folk though they may be, know nothing about, and if it is true also that the only hope for humanity on this planet is an increase in the number of people whose lives are ruled by the mind and spirit of Christ, then surely evangelism is the most urgent task in the world, and the supreme duty of the Christian.

That does not mean that you've got to start dashing about all over the country sharing in rather emotional revival meetings. It is much more likely to mean that you take on the job of caring for half a dozen children in the Sunday-school, and equipping yourself for that high vocation by regular attendance at a Teacher Training Class. Or it may mean running a weekday activity of some sort with a score of boisterous noisy youngsters, setting yourself deliberately to the task of so knowing them and so caring for them that you literally love and pray them into the Kingdom. On any reckoning, the most effective evangelism is that which is done in quiet, unspectacular fashion by faithful men and women whose names never hit the headlines.

But what about all those young people who refuse to join a club which is in any way associated with a Church? How may they be reached and won? Some of them may be members of what are called 'secular' (though a fairer word would be 'non-Church') youth clubs. It may be God's will that some of you should join such clubs with a definite evangelistic intention. That does not mean, of course, that you will walk about accosting people with the impertinent question, 'Are you saved?'—but it does mean that you will offer a living demonstration of Christian ways of talking, working, playing and living together, and that you will be ready to seize the opportunity, when it comes, of Christian witness and testimony.

William Temple used to say that every Church youth club should have its witness team as ready to offer Christian testimony in a non-Church club as its football team is ready to meet members of such a club on the field. And both teams, he added, needed regular and appropriate training.

And what about those young people who never join an organization at all? The only way in which they are likely to be influenced is as they meet Christian people at work or at leisure; the only evangelism by which they are likely to be won is personal evangelism.

I once knew a London office where standards of conversation, honesty and personal relationships were as poor as they well could be. Into that office there came a Christian girl. When the others discovered that she was a Christian, they said they didn't want 'any holy people around,' and they did their best to shock her, hoping she would leave. But she refused to be shocked; she never rebuked them, never preached at them, but just went on living her own joyous radiant Christian life. As time went on the whole atmosphere of that office changed; one by one they sought her out to inquire the secret of her peace and joy, and three of them eventually became members of the Church she attended.

It is essential, of course, that our lives commend our profession. People will be influenced far more by what we are than by what we say. The greatest need of the Church is the need, not of orators or scholars or organizers, but of saints. And saints, remember, are not anæmic figures in stained-glass windows with halos round their heads, still less are they dreary pious people who spend their time condemning the sins of others; they are vital red-blooded men and women who play a full part in the world's affairs, but demonstrate in their every deed and relationship the grace of Christ and the love of God.

20. QUITE GROWN UP

In one of the early pages of this book it was remarked that it was the chief business of the adolescent to stop being one, and I have said a good deal about the various adjustments teenagers have to make as they achieve adult attitudes to their home, their job, their friends of the opposite sex and to society at large.

Does there come a time, ever, when we can claim to be fully adult? When are we quite grown up?

Some people, of course, never do grow up; in one way or another they remain children all their lives. Perhaps most of us tend to be a little childish at times.

Growing up is much more than a matter of physical development. That is something which we can do very little about. Heredity seems to decree for everybody an ultimate size and shape, and in spite of the advertisements in the women's papers, it is very difficult to modify one's physical destiny. By about the eighteenth birthday the human skeleton ceases to grow and we may then be physically mature. But adulthood involves much more than physical development; it implies also intellectual, emotional and social maturity.

Much could be written on these questions. Here let it be sufficient to say that a person who is intellectually mature is one who is able to make up his own mind without being too much influenced by the opinion of others, he has cultivated wide interests, he knows how to employ his leisure time creatively, and he has found a point of view and what might be called a philosophy of life.

The person who is emotionally mature is not easily upset over trifles, he has achieved normal adult relationships with members of the opposite sex, he can accept criticism without hurt feelings, he can make his own decisions, he can accept unpleasant situations without running away from them, and he has a sense of humour. Above all, perhaps, he does not entertain an exaggerated sense of his own importance.

The person who is socially mature can get on with most other people in the ordinary relationships of life, he can take part in the work of a group without trying either to dominate it or to withdraw from it, and he is tolerant to people whose views or customs differ from his own.

Judged by these standards most of us will feel that we still have quite a way to go before we could claim to be quite grown up.

Even this, however, is not all. The really adult person has matured religiously as in all other ways. The real truth about non-religious people is that, however excellent they may be, they have not yet grown up. They are suffering from arrested development. They have left out one whole area of experience. Without faith in God and an awareness of His presence in our lives we remain half-grown, incomplete.

This does not mean, of course, that all religious people are mature adults. Far too many begin the Christian life satisfactorily with an act of decision or an experience of conversion, and seem never to proceed beyond that point. In religion, they remain permanent children. A university vice-chancellor said not long ago that he was 'frightened by the number of young people who come up to the universities today with their minds firmly shut, bolted and barred in religious matters'.

In the New Testament we are called to 'perfection'. This is a word which has troubled many people and perplexed others, but part of its meaning, at least, is 'adult'. When we are told to seek after perfection, we are being told to keep on growing. In religion, as in every other field of knowledge and experience, there is much yet to discover and make our own.

Let me close with a quotation from the Epistle to the Ephesians, in Mr J. B. Phillips's translation:

'His gifts were made that Christians might be properly equipped for their service . . . until the time comes when, in the unity of common faith and common knowledge of the Son of God, we arrive at real maturity —that measure of development which is meant by "The fulness of Christ".'—

Keep on Growing.

FOR FURTHER READING

If you have enjoyed this booklet and would now like to go farther, the following books will take you the next steps.

For Christian Beginners   By L. P. Barnett.
> 16 chapters of plain, down-to-earth guidance and challenge for young Christians.

Menu For Today   By P. Stewart May
> Daily Bible readings for three months.

Prayer Diary For Youth   By L. P. Barnett.

Staying the Course   By Eric G. Frost.
> For thoughtful young Christians who want to 'keep on growing'.